The Nature of
Freedom

GRAHAM COOKE

A DEVOTIONAL WORKBOOK

BOOK 1
THE LETTERS FROM GOD SERIES

Brilliant
BOOK HOUSE

WWW.BRILLIANTBOOKHOUSE.COM

BRILLIANT BOOK HOUSE
PO Box 871450
Vancouver, WA, 98687

This book and all other materials published by Graham Cooke are available online at BrilliantBookHouse.com

If you would like more information on Graham Cooke and his ministry, please visit GrahamCooke.com

Layout by Fast Forward Creative Agency, www.FastForwardCreative.com

ISBN: 978-0-9896262-4-8

ACKNOWLEDGMENTS

Grateful thanks to long time friend Allison Bown for her input into the exercises and assignments.

DEDICATION

To our Tuesday community, Theresa and I love you guys and our times of exploring Jesus.

CONTENTS

INTRODUCTION

We are all on a journey that is inextricably linked to the story of who God wants to become for us. Our journey is not just about our destination but also concerns how we engage with the Lord in the context of His involvement in all of life's situations and processes.

He is eternally joyful, generous, loving, kind, patient and good. We are in the process of learning to become as unchanging as He is.

This book is written in the first person. The idea is that if God were sitting with you in your personal space with Him, what would He most want you to know about this life He chooses to live in you?

How does He see you, think about you and relate to you? How would He speak and connect with every area of your life?

This is the first volume in a series entitled Letters from God... because a passionate Father wants to engage with you in a transformational way.

PREPARATION FOR A DIVINE CONVERSATION

You are about to engage with the passionate heart of God.

Take time to sit, read and listen to what God desires to say to you and hear the resonant kindness, gentleness and passion in His voice.

Pay attention to what rises up in your heart towards Him: gratitude, astonishment, relief, joy, affirmation and possibly the desire to tell Him, "I knew life with You could be like this!" He loves to hear those words.

Embrace the challenges to your previous mindsets. Is this who you've known God to be—or is there a new experience of Him that emerges as you read?

Is there anything that surprises you? It's okay to be perplexed (Acts 10:17-20) but remember, God is not the author of confusion, we are. In our walk with the Lord He is always teaching us how to think because that is the definitive key to growth (Proverbs 23:7, Romans 12:2, I Corinthians 2:12-16). When He challenges our thinking, He creates an opportunity for us to unlearn something so that we are no longer stuck.

Think about the consequences for God in the truth that He lays before you. If He gives you a command, a promise or permission then He has to act towards you in the same context as you, so that together you can explore the truth that sets you free.

For example, if He gives you permission to "Even so, consider yourself to be dead to sin but alive to God in Christ Jesus" (Romans 6:11), this impacts on Him and His relationship with you because He also must consider you dead, which means He cannot work on the old man or be sin conscious towards you!

He loves consequences and joyfully binds Himself to them for our sake.

Consider the questions of exploration that are embedded in these letters. They will help unwrap your thinking, expand your heart and consider your responses.

When you receive a letter from a dear friend, you don't respond with an academic paper! So throughout this journal, there are invitations to craft a letter to God to capture your thoughts about His thoughts—your feelings about His passion and compassion for you.

We keep precious letters from our loved ones and pore over them again and again. That's a great way to approach this journal. As you read and reread His letters to you, explore them more deeply.

Always ask, "What are the key truths here?"

"What aspects of God's nature are being revealed to me?"

"Who does He want to be for me in this situation?"

"What are the key breakthroughs in these truths?"

"What obstacle can you overcome with these truths?"

"What new part of your identity did you discover in this dialogue?"

When God presents us with truth He is inviting us to upgrade our relationship with Him. If you lived in this upgrade what would change for you? Take time out to write and reflect on it.

What are you discovering that you would like to explore further? What interaction with the Lord is available that you may not have considered before or you are now considering in a fresh way?

How is God's presence more real to you through these letters? Write a short statement and include a real world example of how you are engaging Him differently.

Love the learning. If what you read clashes with your perception of truth, be a good Berean (Acts 17:10-11) and search for the truth without prejudice.

There is no transformation outside of a renewed mind. Enjoy the journey into thinking differently and being with God in a fresh way.

The Nature of

Freedom

Graham Cooke

IT'S OVER... SOMETHING GOT FINISHED BEFORE YOU STARTED

Key Scriptures: Revelations 13:8, Genesis 1:26, John 19:30, Romans 6:3-11

Beloved, when We created mankind, the greatest possible gift that We could bestow was freedom. In order for you to be free to choose your way, We had to remove control as a possibility for your life. The essence of control is limitation; the curbing of free will and the repression of the individual. If you are to be fully made in Our image then you must have the same freedom.

We knew that freedom of choice would take some people away from Our loving lifestyle. We do not wish to control anyone or anything, but rather We want to walk people through life situations and be in charge of the process of redemption. With that in mind, before the introduction of light We made a decision that Jesus would become Emmanuel and save people from their sins by taking their place in sacrifice.

In due time He fulfilled that purpose perfectly and here you are with Us! Before you were born your redemption was already completed. Not just the freedom and forgiveness from sin and self-destruction, but also the elimination of all forms of negativity in heart and mind. Anxiety, fear, panic, worry, all forms of dread and every negative thought, emotion, word and deed. True liberation.

On the Cross you were in My mind, heart and vision. I could see the total freedom that death would bring to you. Your death as part of My death. My life for yours. Your new life lived in a joyful partnership of learning and becoming.

1

BREAKING THE MOLD

In My eyes your old life has already met its demise and is finished. The Cross has set you free from your old man; a sin nature and a selfish lifestyle. When I died, so did you. I did not just die for you, I died as you.

When I was buried I took your old man with me and when I was raised from the dead I left your old man behind. He cannot ever be resurrected. It is gone, finished, forever. You died in Me, then a new version of you was raised from the dead through My glorious workings.

Now you and I are walking together in a completely new and totally different life.

Your old self was crucified with Me so that everything connected to that life could never make it past the grave. We are united together always and no one and nothing can ever separate us. Beloved, I am so excited that We are together as resurrected beings. All the old has passed away and you are My new creation in Jesus.

I give you the beautiful, always amazing Holy Spirit to empower and support all your learning as you experience My life in you.

You are no longer a slave to sin. It is no longer your nature. I have removed it. All that remains is your attachment through memory to a habit, which can be broken by our partnership and relationship. He who is dead is entirely free and I will teach you and show you the reality and the power of that freedom.

CONSEQUENCES!

Think of the consequences of you being united with Me both in death and resurrection. It would be utterly absurd for Me to kill your old nature, then also raise it from the dead and try to change it in life!

That would make Me massively double minded. I killed your sinful nature then I brought it back? The people who take your household trash away every week...have they ever brought it back? I know, that makes me smile too. Me, the Lord of the Universe going to these elaborate lengths to put all your sin on My Son, give Him a totally gruesome death, have Him be in hell for three days, resurrect Him to newness of life and at the same time resurrect you to live the same life from the old nature. What would be the point of that? It would make the Cross of Jesus of no effect. It would grossly, insanely undermine His wonderful sacrifice.

Did I punish Jesus enough for sin? Did I judge Him one hundred percent for sin? Did I expend every last ounce of anger, wrath and indignation upon Him for sin? When He took the sins of the whole world upon Himself, He became a loathsome thing to Me. So abhorrent, I turned away from Him and left Him to His shame and humiliation. I condemned Him so that you may become the Beloved.

My dear one, would We go through all that horror and then raise your sinful nature from the grave in order to work on your behavior? If He has dealt with sin once and for all, how then can I remain sin conscious?

If I were dealing with your sinfulness now it would be because I had no faith that Jesus dealt with it in His own body on the tree. For Me to shame or condemn you for your lifestyle choices when

Jesus has already taken that form of punishment in your place...is that not a violation of My agreement with Him?

I absolutely, implicitly believe in the sacrifice of My Son. I will never deny His slaughter by allowing you to feel helpless, hopeless, guilty or condemned. You are free!

Enjoy working with the Holy Spirit to live in the new man, who is Christ within. As you learn to be made in Our image, all your mistakes in that process of becoming are covered by the power of the blood and the Cross.

PRESENT-PAST AND PRESENT-FUTURE

Do you believe what I believe about you being in Christ now? When you think of the old self you must use the past tense and not the present. Our language is clear. You have been buried. You have been united with Him in death. Your old self was crucified, the body of sin was done away with. The one who has died (you) is free now!

When you think of the new, true, resurrected you in Christ you must use a present-future tense to mark the current place you hold in Our affection and to connect you with the life We are cultivating in you for the rest of your days.

Knowing this, you will become like Him in real life. It is Our purpose and We love it! Certainly you shall be made in His likeness. It is a done deal in Our hearts. You have Our undivided attention in Him. You are freed and We believe that you can and will live in Him in total fullness, with Our full help and support.

We therefore give you absolute permission to consider yourself to be dead to sin and to become fully alive to God in Christ Jesus! Beloved, there are necessary, joyful and wonderful consequences for you in believing the truth about yourself. Know this, We joyfully bind ourselves to the same consequences!

That means I can only think of you in one way. You are My Son. I placed you in Him. He also lives in you by His own desire, delight and purpose. I AM is working on making you in the likeness of My Son. Every day, in each circumstance, you are being trained to live from your new man, not the old. When you realize who you are in Him and who He is for you, that oneness and unity breaks every power against you.

I trust the sacrifice of My Son. I judged Him, sentenced Him, punished Him and hold Him executed so that I would never have to do that to you. The power of sin is destroyed; righteousness now reigns in its place. That is what you are practicing in My beautiful Holy Spirit.

Beloved, it makes no sense for Me to be sin conscious if My Son has destroyed sin by His death! I am single minded about you loving holiness. I am totally focused on Christ in you. I concentrate daily on elevating the new man in you to the place of loving acceptance. My heart is fixed on the new, true you in Jesus. I am not double minded about that! You have My permission to be fully alive in Me.

Come on this journey with Me. Leave behind the places where you are stuck. Love the learning. Don't worry if it clashes with your tradition. "You have heard it said, but now I say to you," is a familiar term used by My Son in His ministry. It will become familiar to you also.

Let's get started.

QUESTIONS FOR DIALOGUE

Before each of these response sections, you may want to pause and reread "Preparation for a Divine Conversation" at the beginning of this journal to refresh your heart and mind in how God sees these exchanges.

Consider these key truths:

"Your old self was crucified with Me so that everything connected to that life could never make it past the grave."

1. Where have you carried old self habits into your new life in Christ?

_____

_____

_____

_____

_____

_____

_____

_____

_____

_____

_____

_____

_____

_____

_____

_____

_____

_____

2. What have you believed about yourself that caused you to think or act like that?

_____

_____

_____

_____

_____

_____

_____

_____

_____

_____

_____

_____

_____

_____

_____

_____

_____

_____

_____

_____

_____

_____

_____

_____

_____

_____

_____

_____

_____

3. Who does God desire to be to you in that place?

_____

_____

_____

_____

_____

_____

_____

_____

_____

_____

_____

_____

_____

_____

_____

_____

_____

_____

_____

_____

_____

_____

_____

_____

_____

_____

4. Write a statement about what the consequences for God means for you.

_____
_____
_____
_____
_____
_____
_____
_____
_____
_____
_____
_____
_____
_____
_____
_____
_____
_____
_____
_____
_____
_____
_____
_____
_____
_____

"Do you believe what I believe about you being in Christ now?"

1. Listen to your language in conversations. Is it more past than present or future tense? Filled with grace or failure? Are you as kind towards yourself as God is towards you?

_____

_____

_____

_____

_____

_____

_____

_____

_____

_____

_____

_____

_____

_____

_____

_____

_____

_____

_____

_____

_____

_____

_____

_____

2. What are the upgrades in your language that will reflect what God believes about you? "Instead of saying _____, I can now say _____."

_____

_____

_____

_____

_____

_____

_____

_____

_____

_____

_____

_____

_____

_____

_____

_____

_____

_____

_____

_____

_____

_____

_____

_____

_____

_____

_____

"You have absolute permission to consider yourself to be dead to sin and to become fully alive to God in Christ Jesus.... My heart is only fixed on the new, true you in Jesus."

1. Make a list of personal negatives. Find an opposite for each in the nature of God. Discard the negatives. Example: Worry into peace.

_____

_____

_____

_____

_____

_____

_____

_____

_____

_____

_____

_____

_____

_____

_____

_____

_____

_____

_____

_____

_____

_____

_____

_____

2. These opposites are God's focus. What would change for you if it was your only focus too?

_____

_____

_____

_____

_____

_____

_____

_____

_____

_____

_____

_____

_____

_____

_____

_____

_____

_____

_____

_____

_____

_____

_____

_____

_____

_____

INVITATION TO RESPOND

You've just read a beautiful letter that has touched your heart. Now it is your opportunity to write back. What would you say in response? Keys open us up to God's passion to create truth in us.

What was the most valuable key truth for you and why?

Enjoy writing a short letter to God about your key truth. What did you learn about Him? How did that affect you? Do this with every key truth. God would love it as much as you!

_____
_____
_____
_____
_____
_____
_____
_____
_____
_____
_____
_____
_____
_____
_____
_____
_____
_____
_____
_____
_____
_____
_____

Graham Cooke

WHAT THE CROSS MEANS FOR YOU AND ME

Key Scriptures: Romans 6, Galatians 2:19-21, John 14:19, Ephesians 2:13-15, Romans 8:28, 1 Corinthians 15:31, Colossians 2:13-14

Beloved, We abide with you in both the present and the future. Our intention is to teach and develop you to live in Us now! All your life circumstances, all of them, no matter how hard, grievous or oppositional can be turned around for your good and for your growth in Us.

GOODNESS STARTS HERE

We do not cause these painful moments. Some of them happen because of choices by yourself or people around you. Others come from issues affecting your nation, city, and place of work. The number of things that can cause health issues are huge. We control none of these things. However, We do take charge as you lean into Us and practice your identity in Jesus. In every situation there are two conditions for you to fulfill as We walk you through life.

Firstly, that you practice your love for Us in allowing Us to make you in Our image. That is, learn to stand with Us as We make adjustments to your character, thinking, lifestyle and trust.

Secondly, that you interpret your current situation in the light of your calling and Our purpose for you in the Kingdom. For a regular soldier to become a special forces warrior requires a lot of situational training, better response times, clearer thinking and a willingness to endure.

To overcome evil with good, you must see goodness as a high calling and you must train for it in all the circumstances in life.

Humanity is responsible for freedom and right choices. As We live in you and you abide in Us you become more aware and stronger in faith. Your favor begins to assert itself as you grow in obedience and authority.

POWER TO PREVAIL

Life in fullness brings you to a life lived above your circumstances and not beneath them. Being in Christ enables you to have victory in the present but also to learn to walk with Us and be ready for the future that is already here or close by. You learn by the Spirit to look ahead and plan longer term. You also realize that some situations cannot be resolved in a few days or weeks. In those circumstances your development is part of a long-term program of upgrading your identity and cultivating the trust, wisdom and growth necessary to becoming an overcomer.

Our real passion, though, is to eventually combine present victory with ongoing overcoming, and produce in you the identity of being "more than a conqueror." Beloved, there are some battles that are won by absolute majesty. This is not just Us fighting for you but also you partnering with Us in a dynamic way that causes the enemy not to risk his resources in a conflict with you.

That all sounds wonderfully important and grand, doesn't it? And so it is! After all, you cannot be in Christ and be ordinary, right? You cannot be filled with the Spirit and be mediocre. We are making you like Us! We are amazing.

FUTILITY OF FULLNESS?

The starting place for all of this is the Cross and how We see it in the context of the Kingdom being in you and around you. It is utterly impossible for you to live in fullness from the old nature. There is no power in Heaven or Earth that can fully change your sin nature into a new nature. Your old man was too bad to be cleansed, it had to be crucified. If transformation is only concerned with behavior modification, then Jesus needn't have died. The action of trying to change yourself by your own efforts and asking Us to help you with that can only ever produce futility.

We successfully proved that man trying to keep the rules of behavior (the law) could never work outside of sacrifice. You cannot please Me by trying to please Me! On the Cross I crucified your old nature with Christ. It is dead and buried and therefore no longer a core part of who you are. It is now Christ that lives in you and We are teaching you how to be one with Him; how to see, think, speak and act in line with the real, true you that is born again in Christ. Your spirit lives in Him and He in you. In His sacrifice I abolished forever the law of rules and trying harder, and the shame and condemnation that I so despise.

In My Son, I bring you and Him together to make one new person. It's no longer just you but Him also, and in this life you have peace with Me. Your faith in My Son in you is what pleases Me the most. Do you trust Me when I say that I have made an end of the old you and that I am only working on the new you in Jesus?

Because He lives you live also, but only in Him, never in your old self. We are not renewing your old nature. Cleaning up the old man is like giving a dead person plastic surgery. Death to self was accomplished for you by My Son on the Cross. When you die daily or crucify the flesh you are simply agreeing with the fact of what He accomplished for you. In that context, death to self is not an action on your part but a consequence of you believing in what He accomplished.

That becomes a joyful confession of who We have made you, alive in God through Jesus. By practicing the new, the old remains dead. Life in Jesus compounds the death of the old you. It makes My heart so deliriously happy when I see what My beloved Son has done for you. Now, you are in Him and I see you only in Him and through Him.

Did you ever think of what the consequences are for Me, as His Father, in putting you in My beloved Son and in putting Him in you? I can never see you in any other way! This is wonderful to me! I cannot praise Him enough for what My Son did for Me on the Cross. He gave Me back My dream of having a perfect relationship with My people. He restored you to Me in Himself! Now nothing can ever separate you from who I AM for you. There is no dividing wall because two have become one. By His blood you have peace with Me even while you are learning, failing, growing and changing.

NOTHING'S WRONG; SOMETHING'S MISSING

My consequences of this amazing, selfless act of love involve never having to look at your old man ever again. Now I only get to work with Jesus in your new man. That means Beloved, that when

I look at you I do not see anything wrong with you. Everything that was wrong about you I have canceled out with your death on the Cross. That great list of all that you have done and all that you are not was nailed to the Cross and was taken away in Christ.

Beloved, I do not see anything wrong with you—only what is missing from your experience of Me, and I am totally committed to giving you that encounter and experience. Because you are dead in Christ I can't see anything wrong with you since you are now alive in Christ. There is no sin nature, just a sin habit that will be broken by the new man becoming fully alive and attuned to Jesus. I am not sin conscious, I am righteousness focused in all my dealings. Jesus dealt with sin; the Holy Spirit is dealing with the righteousness of Christ in you. My only involvement with the old nature is to confirm to you that it is dead, and to give you permission to consider it as a fact.

Something is missing rather than something is wrong. Doesn't that sound so much healthier for you? It puts you into a clean, clear, comfortable place in My love for you. This means when the Holy Spirit puts His finger on something that is not yet working properly in your life, He is actually pointing to the site of your next miracle. He is declaring your next upgrade in Christ to you.

So, if He touches an anxiety that is still a habit in you He will declare to you what is missing, which would be peace. The upgrade of peace is the missing part, which replaces anxiety, which is already dead and buried. He turns sorrow into joy, inferiority into confidence. Instead of shame He gives you a double portion of favor. Humiliation is replaced by jubilation.

Unrighteous anger (anger at people) is replaced by gentleness. Beloved, I do not want you working on a negative. I want you to focus with Me on the opposite. I am asking you to move in the opposite spirit. The real problem with negativity is that you have not yet replaced it with something wonderful that represents My nature. In anger, the issue from My perspective is that you are resisting the grace to be gentle.

Above all, I want you to enjoy the process of being transformed by the renewing of your mind. Think like Me and enjoy growing up into the place in Me that it takes you. Freedom is simple. Stop laboring on the old you and join Me in only working on the new, true, real you in Jesus.

Are you ready?

QUESTIONS FOR DIALOGUE

Consider these key truths:

"We do not cause these painful moments... We control none of these. However, We do take charge as you lean into Us and practice your identity in Jesus."

1. What is a current situation in which you are learning to lean into God?

_____

_____

_____

_____

_____

_____

_____

_____

_____

_____

_____

_____

_____

_____

_____

_____

_____

_____

_____

_____

2. Where can you see God's goodness for you in it?

_____

_____

_____

_____

_____

_____

_____

_____

_____

_____

_____

_____

_____

_____

_____

_____

_____

_____

_____

_____

_____

_____

_____

_____

_____

_____

_____

_____

_____

3. What freedom does that bring in how you think about this circumstance?

_____

_____

_____

_____

_____

_____

_____

_____

_____

_____

_____

_____

_____

_____

_____

_____

_____

_____

_____

_____

_____

_____

_____

_____

_____

_____

_____

_____

"Life in fullness brings you to a life lived above your circumstances and not beneath them."

1. How can God help you to live above your life situation?

_____

_____

_____

_____

_____

_____

_____

_____

_____

_____

_____

_____

_____

_____

_____

_____

_____

_____

_____

_____

_____

_____

_____

2. If you practiced that lifestyle what could change in you?

_____

_____

_____

_____

_____

_____

_____

_____

_____

_____

_____

_____

_____

_____

_____

_____

_____

_____

_____

_____

_____

_____

_____

_____

_____

_____

_____

_____

_____

"The Cross redeems you from performance and self effort."

1. What would relaxing into the new man change in you?

2. How does the reality of Christ in you set you free from trying and failing?

_____

_____

_____

_____

_____

_____

_____

_____

_____

_____

_____

_____

_____

_____

_____

_____

_____

_____

_____

_____

_____

_____

_____

_____

_____

_____

_____

_____

_____

_____

3. God can only see Christ in you. How does that feel?

"When I look at you, I do not see anything wrong with you—only what is missing from your experience of Me and I am totally committed to giving you that encounter and experience."

1. How does it feel to know He sees nothing wrong in you? Write a defining statement for yourself to enjoy.

_____

_____

_____

_____

_____

_____

_____

_____

_____

_____

_____

_____

_____

_____

_____

_____

_____

_____

_____

_____

_____

_____

_____

2. What do you love about a God who doesn't find fault in you but instead loves who you are becoming?

_____

_____

_____

_____

_____

_____

_____

_____

_____

_____

_____

_____

_____

_____

_____

_____

_____

_____

_____

_____

_____

_____

_____

_____

_____

_____

_____

_____

3. What would you say is missing in your experience of the new man?

_____

_____

_____

_____

_____

_____

_____

_____

_____

_____

_____

_____

_____

_____

_____

_____

_____

_____

_____

_____

_____

_____

_____

_____

INVITATION TO RESPOND

Write your next letter to Him about your desire and excitement to pursue the missing pieces.

_____

_____

_____

_____

_____

_____

_____

_____

_____

_____

_____

_____

_____

_____

_____

_____

_____

_____

_____

_____

_____

_____

_____

_____

_____

_____

_____

_____

_____

Graham Cooke

YOUR REAL LIFE IS CREATED FROM YOUR AWARENESS OF ME!

Key Scriptures: Colossians 3:1-3, Philippians 3:12-15, Romans 6:13, 2 Corinthians 13:4, John 16:13-15, Matthew 11:25-30

My dear one, being alive to Me in everything means everything to Me! I love walking with you through life. You miss Me when you focus from the old nature. Let Me say again, I am not double minded. I only focus on the new man in Jesus. I cannot—indeed, will not—talk to you or help you with the old nature. To do so would dishonor My beloved Son.

BECOMING ATTUNED TO ME

When you operate from the old you, you are engaged in Failure Mode (FM), when you live in the new man you are involved with Abiding Mode (AM). I AM is attuned to AM not FM. So many times you pray like a widow in FM when you could pray like a Bride in AM. You must tune into what My Son has accomplished, and what the amazing Holy Spirit is training you to become in Me.

Beloved, he that is dead is free from sin. Dead people do not struggle, they rest in peace. That is why when you are overcome by a negative perception from the old nature, you must stop and ask yourself, "Which self is talking here? Is this the old man or is this my new man in Christ?"

That question is territorial. It closes down a place that can never be helpful to you and opens you up to the One Person who knows you best and loves you the most! Asking that question opens you to a powerful consequence in the Spirit that engages you to receive something **now** in Christ.

Being alive to God means that all of your focus is towards Me in every circumstance of life. I will empower the new man to keep moving forward into deeper places in Who I AM for you.

Maturity takes time. It's a long road but a fabulous journey. Do not get so hung up on the destination that you forget to enjoy the life journey with Me. I plan to love and enjoy all My dealings with you in the new man. How could I not? The new man is Christ in you. I adore working with Him so it follows that I will adore being with you in everything. This is My dream. To make you in My image.

YOUR PERSONAL ODYSSEY

Sure, the journey will be difficult at times. It's not easy to train as a soldier. It's not nice to be persecuted. Learning to walk by faith cannot be achieved by logic or it wouldn't be faith. There is so much anxiety in the world that learning to trust requires peace, not endless speculation. If you live in your circumstances then you have chosen a path that is not smooth but full of stones.

My beautiful Holy Spirit is not only your personal trainer but your Comforter for the days when you get off track with the new man. It will take a process of abiding to empower you to stop defaulting to a negative or to the old nature. There is no shame or condemnation in Me. No need to beat yourself up for making a mistake. Relax, rest in Me. Pick yourself up, shrug off the old, put on the new, smile, grin, take My hand, start where you left off. My yoke is easy and My burden is light.

Beloved, if you want to know Me as Father then you must learn to love being a much loved child. If you want to grow up as a mature son you must love being in and with My beloved Son. If you want to be fully equipped and know how I see, think, speak and act, you must love your personal trainer, the genius Holy Spirit. We are here for every eventuality. You must tune into us on I AM.

Press into us using your life situation. Your awareness of Our passion for you, creates life, love and laughter in you regardless of circumstances.

ABUNDANT EXPECTATION

Pay attention to what you are learning and who you are becoming. Nothing in Christ is accidental or incidental. We are working to a plan that is not static or fully predetermined. It lives and breathes in you and around your life situations and choices, keeping you on course and restoring you to the path if you wander off it.

Remember Beloved, redemption is a constant part of your story and restoration is an amazing part of your journey. I AM your North Star, unchanging, ever present and permanently passionate about you regardless of your own inconsistency.

The past is behind you. Let it go as you reach forward. Do not make future decisions based on past experiences. If it was a negative that wounded you...come to Me now! Do not carry it forward. Forget what lies behind you. There is a prize in front of you that keeps releasing new things to you as you connect with the expectation of My Son.

A young child, when learning to walk, gathers bumps and bruises when falling over. Tears come; tears go because they are temporary. Joy is everlasting. A young child does not have the capacity to decide not to walk anymore because the process is hurtful. There is a curiosity, an inherent vibrant expectation that makes them get up with a little help from a comforter and start out again on this journey of life. How can you do less as an adult?

Because We are in you there is an attendant expectation that greater is He who is in you than anything or anyone in the world. Knowing who you are now and who you are becoming next is part of your favor. Using those truths as a navigational aid in Christ will enable you to chart a direction forward into your destiny. The unfolding road map empowers you to travel wisely with purpose. We will provide compass headings such as these plus people and circumstances to help you navigate the journey from present to future in Jesus. This is Our joy!

To be alive in Me means fully engaging with Christ in you. His power is then directed towards you in all your situations. He gives you the stance in your circumstance that enables you to rise up and walk in Him. You learn the best about your new man as you pursue Jesus. The Holy Spirit is the God of discovery, resident within you. He guides you into all truth on this journey. He takes what belongs to Jesus and makes it real to you. He is your internal Spirit of wisdom and revelation.

Expectancy is expected from you. It is compulsory in the Kingdom. We are full of joyous hope for you. If you need a miracle it is because one is available. All of your life circumstances will now point you to the new man and Our Presence in you creating that place of joyful faith and loving trust.

My people can only remain prisoners because they are ignorant of their freedoms. We want you to give us the pre-eminence in all things. Not because We need it, but because it is better for you. Our goal is to empower you to identify Jesus as your source for everything so that you may determine by the Spirit your own identity in Him.

Identity is the key to transformation. You don't become a new person by changing your behavior. You discover the person you already are in Christ and act accordingly. That is what it means to be alive in Me. You cannot see My glory through the eyes of the old man.

The consequences for Me are huge here. It means that I have to be constantly available to the new man. My own expectancy can be constantly activated on your behalf. It is called blessing, favor, permission and promise. I AM joyfully bound to the consequences of truth even as you are!

Please ask Me in line with Christ for the next piece of your provision. Seek the fullness of inner truth in Christ, be curious and expectant of what We will be and do for you. Knock on the Door that is always open. You are welcome. Come in and find what you most need.

Enter into the joyful relationship between the Father, Son and Holy Spirit. You are most welcome!

QUESTIONS FOR DIALOGUE

Consider these key truths:

"When you operate from the old you, you are engaged in Failure Mode (FM). When you live in the new man you are involved with Abiding Mode (AM)...When you are overcome by a negative perception from the old nature, you must stop and ask yourself, 'Which self is talking here?'"

1. Name some of the thinking and language that holds you back from walking in newness of life.

_____

_____

_____

_____

_____

_____

_____

_____

_____

_____

_____

_____

_____

_____

_____

_____

_____

2. If you were to write a statement of criminal accusation of the old man, what would you say?

_____

_____

_____

_____

_____

_____

_____

_____

_____

_____

_____

_____

_____

_____

_____

_____

_____

_____

_____

_____

_____

_____

_____

_____

_____

_____

_____

_____

_____

_____

3. How is the new man better than the old?

_____

_____

_____

_____

_____

_____

_____

_____

_____

_____

_____

_____

_____

_____

_____

_____

_____

_____

_____

_____

_____

_____

_____

"Redemption is a constant part of your journey and restoration is an amazing part of this path."

1. List three areas of your life where poor/past experiences are still affecting present lifestyle.

_____

_____

_____

_____

_____

_____

_____

_____

_____

_____

_____

_____

_____

_____

_____

_____

_____

_____

_____

_____

_____

_____

_____

_____

2. What are the upgrades/antidotes that God is making available to the new you?

3. Write a statement of how God is going to help you upgrade.

_____

_____

_____

_____

_____

_____

_____

_____

_____

_____

_____

_____

_____

_____

_____

_____

_____

_____

_____

_____

_____

_____

_____

_____

_____

_____

_____

_____

_____

> *"The consequences for Me are huge here. It means that I have to be constantly available to your new man. My own expectancy can be constantly activated on your behalf. It is called blessing, favor, permission and promise."*

1. What is an area of relational upgrade that you currently need?

_____

_____

_____

_____

_____

_____

_____

_____

_____

_____

_____

_____

_____

_____

_____

_____

_____

_____

_____

_____

_____

_____

_____

2. How do you see the new man upgrading your relationship with God?

_____

_____

_____

_____

_____

_____

_____

_____

_____

_____

_____

_____

_____

_____

_____

_____

_____

_____

_____

_____

_____

_____

_____

_____

_____

_____

_____

_____

_____

_____

3. What makes you excited, hopeful and confident about being new in Christ?

_____

_____

_____

_____

_____

_____

_____

_____

_____

_____

_____

_____

_____

_____

_____

_____

_____

_____

_____

_____

_____

_____

_____

4. Explain what the consequences for God actually mean for you in this learning?

_____

_____

_____

_____

_____

_____

_____

_____

_____

_____

_____

_____

_____

_____

_____

_____

_____

_____

_____

_____

_____

_____

_____

_____

_____

_____

_____

_____

_____

INVITATION TO RESPOND

"Maturity takes time. It's a long road but a fabulous journey. Do not get so hung up on the destination that you forget to enjoy the life journey with Me."

Instead of a postcard that says "Wish You Were Here", write a postcard to God rejoicing that He is with you! Choose one great thought in this letter. Thank Him for the clarity that it's bringing to your journey. What are the AM (Abiding Mode) thoughts you're listening to now?

Want to be artistic about it? Find a photograph that reflects your discoveries for the other side of your card.

THIS IS HOW I'M WORKING IN YOU

Key Scriptures: Ephesians 4:20-24, 2 Corinthians 5:14-18, John 14:27, 1 John 4:18, Colossians 3:9-10, Romans 8:1-2

Beloved, your old nature is dead in Christ. I really want you to breathe out a sigh of relief, or break into your happy dance. To Me it means the end of your struggle; no more shame or condemnation, no striving and stress. I AM so delighted to completely set you free from any negative context.

THE LAW OF LIFE

The law is dead to you. The only law you are now subject to is the law of the Spirit of life in Christ Jesus. The law of loving Me and also loving others! No more legalistic pharisseism to live under. You are a new creation. All the old things have passed away. We have made all things new for you and we are actively engaged in showing you what that means for your life.

I love the fact that We have raised you to such a new level of life that you are completely disconnected from the old you. I left nothing to chance here. In Our discussion before the foundation of the world, We agreed that We did not want even a tiny shred of the old man to remain. No leaven whatsoever. We wanted a complete and totally dominant freedom to become your true place of exploration in Us.

Now you are alive in Christ and He in you, it is time for you to have the same relationship with Me as He does! Anything less than that is not the Gospel that He died to give you. The glad tidings of great joy means that great joy must be a key part of our relationship.

THIS IS GOD'S PASSION FOR YOU

If you have never heard the Fullness of the Truth that is in Jesus, then you are living with an impoverished gospel. I want your freedom. I want you to experience Our delight in you so that you may be delighted in us.

I want your peace to be as huge as Mine. I want your rest to be as dominant as Mine. I desire that the enormous depths of love that I have for My Son should become your lifestyle in Him. I have set My heart on you encountering the laughter of Heaven as your earthly normal. As a new creation I want you to have all the experiences with Me that Jesus was dying to give you!

Because you have been raised to newness of life all Our focus with you becomes the new man. We will only deal with the real you in Christ. This is so exciting for Me.

New things are coming to you and they all originate in Me and come to you through the person of My Son. Your freedom is My passion. Your upgrade is My delight.

Remember, I am not double minded about you. I know that Jesus removed your old man from the scene of your life and replaced it with a new creation. When I look at you now I cannot see anything wrong, only what is missing. I am in the business of strategic life exchange: new for old. I do not require you to work on the old. I just want you to lay it aside as We have when we put it in the grave.

We will teach you to put off the old and put on the new! It begins, Beloved, with a renewed way of thinking. A legalistic mindset would want to improve the old, which is impossible. Death cannot be upgraded. It must be exchanged for the ultimate in advancement, promotion and divine advantage. The life of Jesus in you. This is how it works.

GIVING YOU MY LIKENESS

The Holy Spirit will put His finger on a part of your life that is not working. You will know it because you may feel guilty or even upset about yourself. That's a good sign. Guilt is a friend because it leads you to ask Me questions and seek My heart. Being uneasy or upset is a sign that something good is about to happen. When your old nature is upset it's because I want to exchange it for something new.

I know that some traditions think that these things are a sign for people to work on themselves. The problem is they work on the wrong self. I want you to lay aside the old self and take your thinking about what is happening to a higher place. From there I want you to put on the new self, which is My likeness that I am creating in you.

It works like this: if you are worried or anxious about something then you know that negative mindsets and emotions belong to the old man. What is missing? That would be peace. My peace I give you! Replace anxiety with peace and I will help you to establish peace as the response and the lifestyle that I am elevating in you in Christ.

If you have fears that affect your relationships or life in general, then the Holy Spirit will want to bring freedom. My perfect love casts out fear! The issue surrounding fear is an imperfect relationship with love. There is no fear in love. In a conflict with fear, love wins every time. I am going to focus on you being My Beloved. Not just as a concept to which you can give mental assent.

I want you to have an encounter with My life at that point of need. I want you to engage with Me in receiving new life in that place. When We allow a need to be highlighted in this way it is not to showcase something in you that is wrong. It is to let you know that We have a gift for you! We are going to give you the missing piece. Then We are going to train you in how to keep it, use it and be changed by it. We love to establish truth as a lifestyle.

IT'S A POWERFUL PROCESS

Beloved, We are so going to make you like Us! To do that effectively and lovingly means We cannot ever focus on a sin or a negative that Jesus has already taken away. We are only focused on your new man. Allow that thought to become dominant. That's how you renew your mind. How We think becomes how you think. Real transformation comes through a renewed mind. See it the way We do, think about it from Our level, speak to it in new life just as We do in you.

We are creating a whole new identity in Jesus. What is the truth that sets you free from a sin focused lifestyle? It is this: We do not deal with your old self! We lay it aside. We are not engaged on modifying your behavior. We lay it aside.

We focus on your new man and We engage with your identity in Jesus. Identity is the key to transformation.

- Lay aside the old you by reckoning yourself to be dead.

- Be renewed in how you see and think about your new self. This will involve some rejoicing and thanksgiving!

- See the replacement part that belongs to you in Christ.

- Put on that new part of My nature and character so that your lifestyle is recreated in righteousness of truth.

Know the truth by encounter and it will set you free to experience Me. There are consequences for Me if you partner with the Holy Spirit in this process of strategic life exchange. I have to be in this with you. I cannot leave nor forsake you in the process. We stand together in the same space. I love this! I want to partner with you but you must process in Me and through Me.

You don't have a sin problem. You have a problem with beauty and majesty. You don't realize how beautiful you are to Me and how majestic My love is towards you. My favor is a consequence of my involvement in your upgrade. In every circumstance of your life your new man, My likeness, is staring you in the face. My favor empowers you to step into your new, true identity in Christ.

You are meant to be having hundreds of encounters with the One who adores you. We gave you the Holy Spirit because He is an irrepressible genius, full of life and your personal mentor in all things Jesus. If every single thing in your life is primarily about you being made in My image then you having favor in My eyes is most crucial. Confidence, assurance, belief, hope, vision, anticipation and possibility are all the evidence of My presence in you.

Favor can begin the moment you stop being double minded about how I see you. Would you like to continue on this journey with Me?

Graham Cooke

QUESTIONS FOR DIALOGUE

Consider these key truths:

"The only law that you are subject to is the law of the Spirit of life in Christ Jesus. The law of loving Me and also loving others!"

1. What old self thoughts does this truth set you free from? Make a list.

_____

_____

_____

_____

_____

_____

_____

_____

_____

_____

_____

_____

_____

_____

_____

_____

_____

_____

_____

_____

2. Write a new, brilliant thought for each of these instead.

_____
_____
_____
_____
_____
_____
_____
_____
_____
_____
_____
_____
_____
_____
_____
_____
_____
_____
_____
_____
_____
_____
_____
_____
_____
_____
_____
_____
_____

3. Describe the joy, hope or peace that this statement gives you.

_____

_____

_____

_____

_____

_____

_____

_____

_____

_____

_____

_____

_____

_____

_____

_____

_____

_____

_____

_____

_____

_____

_____

_____

_____

_____

_____

"I want you to have an encounter with My life at that point of need. I want you to engage with Me in receiving new life in that place."

1. Name an aspect of new life that God is offering to you.

_____

_____

_____

_____

_____

_____

_____

_____

_____

_____

_____

_____

_____

_____

_____

_____

_____

_____

_____

_____

_____

_____

_____

_____

_____

_____

2. What is the missing piece it provides?

_____

_____

_____

_____

_____

_____

_____

_____

_____

_____

_____

_____

_____

_____

_____

_____

_____

_____

_____

_____

_____

_____

_____

_____

_____

_____

3. How does experiencing God's delight in you expand your capacity to receive freely?

_____

_____

_____

_____

_____

_____

_____

_____

_____

_____

_____

_____

_____

_____

_____

_____

_____

_____

_____

_____

_____

_____

_____

_____

_____

_____

_____

_____

_____

"There are consequences for Me if you partner with the Holy Spirit in this process of strategic life exchange...I cannot leave nor forsake you in the process. We stand together in the same space. I love this!"

1. What's the encouragement you feel in reading this part of your letter?

_____

_____

_____

_____

_____

_____

_____

_____

_____

_____

_____

_____

_____

_____

_____

_____

_____

_____

_____

_____

_____

_____

_____

_____

2. Are there places that are not working that you feel His finger on?

_____

_____

_____

_____

_____

_____

_____

_____

_____

_____

_____

_____

_____

_____

_____

_____

_____

_____

_____

_____

_____

_____

_____

_____

_____

_____

_____

_____

Graham Cooke

3. What exchanges is the Holy Spirit excited to partner with you in?

INVITATION TO RESPOND

Write a thank you note to God for His gift of a new thing for an old area in your life. Tell Him how you plan to explore it!

_____
_____
_____
_____
_____
_____
_____
_____
_____
_____
_____
_____
_____
_____
_____
_____
_____
_____
_____
_____
_____
_____
_____
_____
_____
_____
_____

Graham Cooke

Graham Cooke

MY EMPOWERING PRESENCE

Key Scriptures: 1 John 4:19, James 1:17, John 3:27, 1 Corinthians 8:6, Ephesians 1:2-8, 1 John 2:1-6, Hebrews 4:16 & 12-15, 1 Corinthians 4:12, 1 Peter 3:9 & 5:10, 2 Peter 3:18

Beloved, grace begins in Heaven not Earth. The starting point for grace is My love for My Son in you. Your beginning is always orchestrated by Me. I initiate, you respond. That is the way salvation began (in Heaven) and therefore the only way that it can be sustained. Beloved, you love Me because I first loved you. Thank you for responding.

EVERYTHING BEGINS WITH GOD, ALWAYS!

Every good thing given and every perfect gift comes down to you from above, from Me. I am the Unchanging One, which means My behavior towards you is based on who I AM not on who you are not.

My demeanor and conduct towards you are based upon My love for My Son in you not on your performance as a believer. I put Him in you and you in Him so you would always have a place of safety as you learn your identity in Him. Grace is your place of safety in Christ.

A person can receive nothing unless it has been given to them from Heaven. Jesus in you is Our gift to you. The Holy Spirit in you is Our gift to you. The grace to walk with them in a habitational lifestyle is Our gift to you. The righteousness required to embrace this new life and learn to walk with a holy God is Our gift to you.

For you there is one God, Me the Father, from whom are all things, and you exist for Me. I have always wanted children. I have always wanted to be a part of watching them grow in grace and learn to be with Me. There is one Lord, Jesus Christ, by whom are all things and you exist through Him. This life you live in Him empowers you to abide with Us.

In Jesus, grace takes you to a high place in your beginning with Him, then elevates you and escalates your walk from there. In Jesus you are blessed with every kind of spiritual blessing that We desire for you.

IN GRACE YOU DISCOVER OUR DELIGHT IN YOU

We are so delighted in Our choice of you to be in Our family. We have always had Our eye on you! Now, in Jesus, you finally belong to Me. There are so many things I want you to have.

They will all come to you as gifts. Your learning is a gift from Me to you. The first think I want you to learn is the kind intention of My will towards you. I am the Unchanging One. The North Star. The One that never leaves. The One who has put My Son in your heart (innermost being) and therefore by doing that, has made your heart My own.

I am your dwelling place and you abide in Me. My plan is to empower you to be both holy and blameless just like Me. It will be exciting and we will have a wild ride on days but as you take My yoke—relationship, partnership and ownership—into you, My rest will smooth out the rough places. Always remember that I love your learning and I am delighted to show you all things in Me, in My timing.

I have ordained that grace will be your teacher too as you learn the beauty and the glory of becoming the Beloved. I will lavish grace upon you because it is the key to redemption by blood and absolute forgiveness. The riches of My grace to you will enable you to become healthy and learn fullness in My abiding presence. Beloved, you cannot go to a higher place in Me without becoming rich in grace.

Grace is a prerequisite, and understanding how grace works is one of the most important pieces of learning in the Kingdom.

WHAT GRACE IS...

Grace can never be separated from My primary purpose, which is Sonship for you. I want sons and daughters, and grace is My chosen means of creating relationship with you. It is the place where you see, know and feel the kind intentions that are huge in My affection for you. Beloved, if grace has not yet become glorious to you it is a sign that you have something immense and precious to discover in our relationship together.

Grace is tied to My own nature and to My desired relationship with you. For that reason grace can never be undeserved favor. I do not give you grace because of who you are or your performance as a Christian. I give you grace because of who I AM and because Jesus lives in you! I give you grace because of Him. He is the new man in you teaching and demonstrating Our relationship together in you.

Grace as undeserved favor is the smallest, weakest, least effective expression of Our nature in you. If grace is undeserved favor then either Jesus never had any or if He did, then He must have done something wrong to be given that type of grace, which would disqualify Him from being your savior!

Grace is My empowering presence within you that enables you to become the person that I see when I look at you.

Beloved, I can only see Jesus in you and you in Him. This is so exciting for Me. I absolutely love the fact that every time I look at you I see Him. When you are doing well and learning properly I see Him. When you are doing badly and learning, I still see Him and I respond to Him in you! That is a grace that is rich towards you.

POOR GRACE IS ALWAYS NEGATIVE!

If I were poor in grace I would live with you according to your behavior. I would use shame and condemnation, anger and judgment to guilt you into change. I would have to withhold love, mercy and goodness until you shaped up. I would have to drop people when they needed Me the most. Turn My back on them when they needed My goodness and kindness to repent. If grace is poor then love would fail. I would have no honor, integrity or righteousness. Righteousness means that I can only see what is right, think, speak and act rightly. I can only do what is right, which is why I attach grace to Jesus in you because He is your life!

When my people live in a false concept of grace they are prone to using hateful language, gossip, rumor, slander, false accusation, lies, or sending people to hell.

QUESTIONS FOR DIALOGUE

Consider these key truths:

"My demeanor and conduct towards you are based upon My love for My son in you, not on your performance as a believer....A person can receive nothing unless it has been given to them from Heaven."

1. How many of God's gifts to you were mentioned in this letter? Write them down.

_____

_____

_____

_____

_____

_____

_____

_____

_____

_____

_____

_____

_____

_____

_____

_____

_____

_____

2. What does it feel like to see such a pile of gifts with your name on them?

_____

_____

_____

_____

_____

_____

_____

_____

_____

_____

_____

_____

_____

_____

_____

_____

_____

_____

_____

_____

_____

_____

_____

_____

_____

_____

3. God placed you in Christ so He could be delighted in you always. What does His delight mean to you?

_____

_____

_____

_____

_____

_____

_____

_____

_____

_____

_____

_____

_____

_____

_____

_____

_____

_____

_____

_____

_____

_____

_____

_____

_____

> *"When you are doing well and learning properly, I see Jesus. When you are doing badly and learning, I still see Him and I respond to Him in you. That is a grace that is rich towards you."*

1. What could be a new thought when you feel you're doing badly?

_____

_____

_____

_____

_____

_____

_____

_____

_____

_____

_____

_____

_____

_____

_____

_____

_____

_____

_____

_____

_____

_____

2. Explain how doing well and badly can both become a great learning opportunity.

_____

_____

_____

_____

_____

_____

_____

_____

_____

_____

_____

_____

_____

_____

_____

_____

_____

_____

_____

_____

_____

_____

_____

_____

_____

_____

_____

_____

_____

_____

"The way I see you empowers you to live shame free, even while you are making mistakes in growing and changing. Your ability to receive forgiveness quickly is vital for your growth. Condemnation wastes time that could be spent on reflecting and learning properly in My Spirit."

1. How could receiving forgiveness quickly accelerate your growth in God?

_____

_____

_____

_____

_____

_____

_____

_____

_____

_____

_____

_____

_____

_____

_____

_____

_____

_____

_____

_____

_____

2. Describe what a shame free life would look like for you.

_____

_____

_____

_____

_____

_____

_____

_____

_____

_____

_____

_____

_____

_____

_____

_____

_____

_____

_____

_____

_____

_____

_____

_____

_____

_____

_____

_____

"Grace steps in when others step out."

1. What current areas of your life would you like grace to step into?

_____

_____

_____

_____

_____

_____

_____

_____

_____

_____

_____

_____

_____

_____

_____

_____

_____

_____

_____

_____

_____

_____

_____

_____

_____

_____

_____

2. Where can you become rich in grace towards others?

_____
_____
_____
_____
_____
_____
_____
_____
_____
_____
_____
_____
_____
_____
_____
_____
_____
_____
_____
_____
_____
_____
_____
_____
_____
_____
_____

3. What would change in your relationship with the Lord if you totally received His grace?

_____

_____

_____

_____

_____

_____

_____

_____

_____

_____

_____

_____

_____

_____

_____

_____

_____

_____

_____

_____

_____

_____

_____

_____

_____

_____

_____

INVITATION TO RESPOND

"Grace is My empowering presence that enables you to become the person that I see when I look at you."

Write a letter to God that expresses what you're seeing about yourself when you look through His eyes of grace. What aspects of the new, true you are becoming more real?

_____

_____

_____

_____

_____

_____

_____

_____

_____

_____

_____

_____

_____

_____

_____

_____

_____

_____

_____

_____

_____

Graham Cooke

Graham Cooke

MY RIGHTEOUSNESS
AND HOW I SEE REPENTANCE

Key Scriptures: 2 Corinthians 5:21, 1 Corinthians 1:30, John 15:1-11, Philippians 4:13, Colossians 1:27, Colossians 2:6 & 3:1-4, John 14:6, 14:17, 15:26, 16:13-15, Matthew11:28-30, Romans 11:35-36, Ephesians 4:14-16, Hebrews 8:6-13, Romans 3:23, 1 John 1:9, Ephesians 4:20-24

Beloved, all of My passion is directed towards you in the person of My beloved Son. I declare that you are righteous because of what He has done on your behalf. I collected all the debts and sins against you. I totaled the full sum of them and placed them all on Him on the Cross. You are free, past, present and future in Him.

LIFE IN THE SPIRIT ALWAYS
STARTS WITH GOD NOT MAN

Now, as you learn to abide in Him it is His righteousness that empowers you to live in the way that only We can! You become the righteousness of God only in Him. You have freedom in your new man to love what We love. Purity, righteousness, loving-kindness and goodness are the environment that we adore. You are welcome into this space with Us!

You are not the initiator in these things. We do not require of you that you take the truth and apply it to your life. Rather, We request that you learn the practice of abiding and dwelling in Him so that His life comes through you.

You are able to do everything through Him because His indwelling presence strengthens your life. It is Christ in you who upgrades all your expectation in walking in Me to the same level of glory that We occupy. You received His life in your new man as a direct replacement for the old life that ended on the Cross. His life and His way becomes your delight. You get to walk in the same passion and desire as He does in His Father.

As one who is raised up from the dead to enjoy the same life as Jesus, let His life rule in you. In Christ you can learn to think from Heaven first rather than try to change your earthly thinking. Beloved, only He can live this life in you. Your life is now hidden in Him. He is your life!

I do not give you a truth and teach you to apply it. Rather, Jesus who is the Way, the Truth and the Life, lives in you and flows through you as you rest in Him. In the same way, the Spirit of Truth lives with you and is always in you. The world cannot receive that truth unless they receive the presence of God. Truth is a person, not just a value or a principle.

THE KINGDOM WORKS LIKE THIS

The Spirit of Truth empowers you to live in the fullness of Christ so that His life flows through you.

Beloved, this is how We work. I give My peace to you but not in the same way as the world gives things. The world would put something into your hands for you to use; a tool, a means for you to apply and use peace. That is not the Kingdom Way, Truth and Life in Jesus.

Instead, We give you presence. We are your peace! The Prince of Peace overcomes all worry, anxiety and trouble. When you are weary and heavy laden it is because you are trying to live this life in your own strength. Come to Us first as your absolute priority. We will give you rest in Ourselves and teach you how to become rest in Us. It is just a simple turning, lifting and yielding of your heart in thanksgiving and gratitude for the supremacy of His life within.

My presence will always be with you, in you and working through you. Who has first given to Me that it may be paid back to him again? No one, Beloved. We are the givers, the Ones who give you life. This life flows from Us, through Us and returns to Us in everything.

All our gifts to you come because of Our presence in you. All the power and grace gifts belong to the Holy Spirit who gives as He wills. The fruit of the Spirit belong to Him and He moves in them through you.

MY RIGHTEOUSNESS, YOUR JOYFUL RESPONSE

Beloved, righteousness is exactly the same. We are righteous in you, for you, to you. He, who never experienced sin, was made sinful on your behalf so that you could become the righteousness of God in Him. You are in Christ by My doing and I have made Him your wisdom, your righteousness, your lifestyle of practical holiness and your full atonement and freedom.

We are not dealing with sin. Jesus dealt with that at Calvary. We are only teaching your new man how to live in Our righteousness. We speak the truth in love to you because We are calling you up to your true identity in Jesus. We do not deal with fear, We become your courage. In anxiety We develop confidence instead. In worry We focus only on peace because it is the antidote to the negative. We do not help you work on your anger, it is dead. Instead We empower you to become gentle. We exchange irritation for patience, bitterness for gratitude and we turn sorrow into joy.

REPENTANCE IS MORE WONDERFUL IN THE NEW COVENANT

The old has passed away. We make all things new and completely different. Repentance in the new covenant is very different than repentance in the old. When people lived under the law they had to make a sacrifice for sin at the temple and they had to repent for what they did that was wrong. The new covenant makes that obsolete because of what Jesus did in Himself in being the sacrifice for sin.

Now that He is our life He engages with God in you so that you are always accepted in the Beloved. Because you are living in the new man you have to learn to repent from that place because the old place of repentance has passed away. A new repentance is here. It works like this:

If you are learning peace in the new man but keep defaulting to your previous habit of anxiety, you cannot repent of your anxiety because Jesus took it away on the cross. Instead, your repentance sounds like this: "Father, thank you for giving me a great opportunity to walk in peace. I repent that I did not practice Your peace and I ask that You give me another occasion soon to upgrade peace in my life." Doesn't that sound so much better? No guilt or shame and no need to condemn yourself. Instead there is a gentle, joyful willingness to realize the potential for the next opportunity and to be ready for it!

In the Old Testament people repented for doing wrong, in the new you can only repent of failing to do what is right in the nature of Jesus. Sin in the new covenant is defined as falling short of My glory. That happens when you do not receive what Jesus died to give you...Himself! He's in your life. When you default to a response that is less than He is for you, repentance that restores you to the upgrade is what is most needed.

Beloved, if you confess that you missed the opportunity to be Christ-like, know that I am faithful and just to forgive you and cleanse you from not doing what is right.

Repentance is your privilege, because in the new man context, it is also a reminder of who you are in Me and who you are becoming by the Spirit. It is not required for you to repent in line with something that I have declared to be dead.

To repent towards your new nature in Jesus fixes your attention on what I am doing now in your present future. In this way you are always moving forward and not looking back. That is so exciting to Me. When you submit to shame and condemnation it is easier for you to step back into default and question your identity in My beloved Son.

Please remember: if you are trying to change your old man behavior and I am developing your new man identity in Christ, you will have a disconnect with My primary purpose. The kind intention of My will is to make you as much like Me as possible in this life so that scripture can be fulfilled, "as He is, so are you in this world."

I absolutely love the process of transforming you. If you love the learning involved in all your circumstances then We will enjoy this process together. Beloved, I am aware that you have not been taught these truths and have not been mentored in My reality. That is why you need to be renewed in the Spirit of your mind. Then you can lay aside the old man and put on the new. In learning with Me you can focus on the identity of the new man and cease defaulting to an old man that was crucified a long time ago.

I am excited about what will happen between us as We walk this road together.

QUESTIONS FOR DIALOGUE

Consider these key truths:

"You are not the initiator in these things. We do not require of you that you take the truth and apply it to your life. Rather, We request that you learn the practice of abiding and dwelling in Him so that His life comes through you."

1. In what way is God taking initiative in your current growth?

_____

_____

_____

_____

_____

_____

_____

_____

_____

_____

_____

_____

_____

_____

_____

_____

_____

_____

_____

2. What old self thoughts does this key truth lock away?

_____

_____

_____

_____

_____

_____

_____

_____

_____

_____

_____

_____

_____

_____

_____

_____

_____

_____

_____

_____

_____

_____

_____

_____

_____

_____

_____

_____

3. What are the new thoughts that it unlocks instead?

_____

_____

_____

_____

_____

_____

_____

_____

_____

_____

_____

_____

_____

_____

_____

_____

_____

_____

_____

_____

_____

_____

_____

_____

_____

_____

_____

_____

_____

_____

_____

"When you are weary and heavy laden, it is because you are trying to live this life in your own strength. Come to Us first as your absolute priority."

1. Think of an area of weariness in your life.

_____

_____

_____

_____

_____

_____

_____

_____

_____

_____

_____

_____

_____

_____

_____

_____

_____

_____

_____

_____

_____

_____

_____

_____

_____

2. Who does God want to be for you in that space?

_____

_____

_____

_____

_____

_____

_____

_____

_____

_____

_____

_____

_____

_____

_____

_____

_____

_____

_____

_____

_____

_____

_____

_____

_____

_____

_____

_____

3. How does it feel to stand with Him, knowing you are welcome there?

_____

_____

_____

_____

_____

_____

_____

_____

_____

_____

_____

_____

_____

_____

_____

_____

_____

_____

_____

_____

_____

_____

_____

_____

_____

_____

_____

_____

_____

"We are righteousness in you, for you, to you!"

1. If you are not allowed to work on the old nature how does transformation occur?

_____

_____

_____

_____

_____

_____

_____

_____

_____

_____

_____

_____

_____

_____

_____

_____

_____

_____

_____

_____

_____

_____

_____

_____

_____

2. How does the Lord demonstrate His righteousness in you?

"The old has passed away. We make all things new and completely different. Repentance in the new covenant is very different than repentance in the old."

1. In what ways is new covenant repentance better than the old?

_____
_____
_____
_____
_____
_____
_____
_____
_____
_____
_____
_____
_____
_____
_____
_____
_____
_____
_____
_____
_____
_____
_____
_____

2. Would new covenant repentance be a different type of experience for you? Describe how.

_____

_____

_____

_____

_____

_____

_____

_____

_____

_____

_____

_____

_____

_____

_____

_____

_____

_____

_____

_____

_____

_____

_____

_____

_____

_____

_____

_____

3. What new freedom do you see for yourself in those differences?

_____
_____
_____
_____
_____
_____
_____
_____
_____
_____
_____
_____
_____
_____
_____
_____
_____
_____
_____
_____
_____
_____
_____
_____
_____

INVITATION TO RESPOND

Write a note responding to God's invitation into peace, joy, courage...whatever it is you are moving towards. What are you most excited about discovering? What do you believe will happen between you as you travel together?

_____

_____

_____

_____

_____

_____

_____

_____

_____

_____

_____

_____

_____

_____

_____

_____

_____

_____

_____

_____

_____

_____

_____

_____

_____

_____

Graham Cooke

AN INVITATION TO COME UNSTUCK

Key Scriptures: Romans 7:14-25, Genesis 18:14, Hebrews 8:6-13, Luke 16:16, Colossians 3:1-4, Philippians 4:13 & 2:13, Romans 6:7, Galatians 2:2, Ephesians 4:22-24, Romans 6:11

Beloved, your life is not how you find it. It is how I make it. I know every pitfall, every difficulty that you will face in the course of your growing up in Me into a place of authority, fullness, maturity, and favor.

The answer to everything is always going to be found in the Person of My Beloved Son. There is no other name or way to be saved outside of Him.

There is no other discipling process in the way of salvation than by the incomparable Holy Spirit who is your Helper, Trainer, and Comforter. No one is more imaginative than your Heavenly Father at creating opportunities for growth and transformation.

Is anything too hard for Me? Is there any situation where I cannot be magnificent towards you? I know how to deal with every eventuality. In truth, you are not much of a challenge to the power of My loving-kindness, goodness, joy, and patience.

LET YOUR EYE BE SINGLE AND FOCUSED

People become stuck because they have not seen what I see. They adhere to a way of thinking that has no outcome except struggle, stress, and perplexity. Mostly it occurs because people can be double-minded about the truth.

They have one foot in the Old covenant and another in the New, trying to reconcile both in their spiritual experience of Me.

We are very clear in Heaven that Jesus was sent to bring an end to one covenant and introduce a better covenant by His own blood and sacrifice. One of My favorite things He preached was: "For all the prophets and the Law spoke until John; since that time, the Gospel of the Kingdom of God has been preached (by Jesus!) and everyone is pressing into it!" I shouted with joy when He proclaimed, "You have heard it said, but now I say!"

It was wonderful watching Him transition My people out of one covenant into another. We had talked for so long together. We had fellowshipped in Our creative imagination about the total freedom that would come to Our beloved people in Christ. I remember the Holy Spirit becoming so excited that He would get up and dance for joy around Us at the thought of helping untold millions of people adjust to Heaven whilst living on Earth.

Beloved, please receive My absolute delight in you. We are overjoyed at being with you, supporting your learning and empowering you to walk with Us as We walk with each other. On Earth as it is in Heaven.

INDWELLING PRESENCE ALWAYS UPGRADES YOUR THINKING

Beloved, you cannot bring old man perception, thinking, and language into a new covenant. You are a new creation, all the old has passed away, everything is different and new in Christ. When people do not know how to walk with Us, they often default to a lesser way of thinking. This can lead them into areas of stress and struggle. They are detained by an impediment in their mindset, which does not allow them to proceed to a place of breakthrough.

People can try to use values and principles to find Me. We love values and principles, but they are best realized by Our Indwelling Presence, not apart from an experience of Our nature. The lack of Presence causes people to ask questions and come to conclusions that are not a legitimate part of being in Christ. Wanting new but thinking old is a sure sign that there is a blockage in the thinking process. People legitimize old thinking and turn it into an aspect of spiritual struggle, where they almost expect to be defeated, and make allowances for being overcome. It is a religious learned helplessness that can never reflect Our Majesty, Sovereignty, and Supremacy. My child, if we are making you in Our image, then you must come up higher, so that like Us, you may see, think, speak, and act from another realm of life. We call it, being seated with Christ in Heavenly places.

Your old man with all those negative thoughts is dead. Your new man is constantly in Our Presence because We are your dwelling place in the Spirit.

We make Our abode in you. We created a habitational culture so that you could live from Heaven to Earth. That is why We want you to set your mind on things above, not on things on the Earth. The person who would entertain earthbound thinking is dead. People who are dead do not struggle, they rest in peace.

BECOMING ALIVE TO WHO GOD IS FOR YOU IS KEY!

I cannot call you out on your old man behavior when I consider it to be dead. To look at you with disapproval would violate the power of Jesus' sacrifice. I have no disappointment, frustration, anger, distrust, or impatience with you. Why? Because your new man is so compelling to Me. I see your freedom always! I am so alive to the new man in My Beloved Son. Why would I settle for less in your experience of Me? I want your fullness to be real and astonishing.

I want you to be awestruck at what We are doing in you! I want you to be so astonished that praise, rejoicing, and thanks flow out of you effortlessly. I want you so overcome with His life that victory is normal, prayer is joyful, difficulties would upgrade you, and nothing would be impossible for you in My Son.

FIVE AREAS OF DISTRESS THAT ARE UNNECESSARY

Beloved, a sinner mindset can only focus on sin. We broke the mold of sin and created in Christ a new man who would rise up in righteousness and purity to become a saint.

The Mind of Christ is only focused on righteousness and truth.

- When the old man says, "The willing is present, but the doing is not," the new man proclaims, "I can do all things in Christ who strengthens me."

- When the performance person says, "The good I want to do, I cannot do," the Holy Spirit says, "God works in you both to will and to do."

- When your old self says, "Sin dwells in me," Jesus says, "He that is dead is freed from sin."

- When the negative one in you says, "I find that evil is present in me," I say, "You have been crucified with Christ; it is no longer you that lives, but Christ lives in you; and the life which you now live in the flesh, you live by faith in the Son of God, who loved you and gave Himself up for you."

- When the captive one says, "I see a different law within the members of my body waging war against the law of my mind and making me a prisoner," We collectively proclaim to you, "Lay aside the old self and be renewed in the spirit of your mind, and put on the new self, which is the likeness of God and has been created in righteousness and holiness of the truth."

ENGAGING WITH PRESENCE PRODUCES A MORE POWERFUL INTERNAL REALITY

Beloved, do not create perception and thinking from scripture that actually disempowers you from experiencing freedom. In Christ, My Presence in you produces a perspective, mindset, and language that allows you to engage with My Kingdom reality. If the truth has not yet set you free, you must find the lie that is binding you and cut the cord. There is no place for mediocrity in My Son.

You must know the difference between what is true in your life-style and what is the Truth in Me. It may be true that you have a sin habit, but the Truth is that you are a new creation in Christ. All the old has passed away and all things are now new.

Your old self looks at behavior and elevates what is merely true into a Truth and finds scripture to fit a perspective that We do not condone. Your new man looks at your identity in Jesus and rejoices in who He is for you.

It is the difference between your state, how you see yourself in the flesh, and your Standing, who you really are in Christ! Beloved, you will only remain a prisoner as long as you are ignorant of your freedom in the Truth. When you identify with My Beloved Son, you see yourself as He sees you. That is what it means to be Alive to God.

The struggle is what you suffer when the old man is alive and running the show. You cannot learn Christ in this way. It is for free-dom that We have set you free. The consequences for you and Me in the Truth are absolutely wonderful.

QUESTIONS FOR DIALOGUE

Consider these key truths:

"Is anything too hard for Me? Is there any situation where I cannot be magnificent towards you? I know how to deal with every eventuality. In truth, you are not much of a challenge to the power of My loving-kindness, goodness, joy and patience."

1. How does it feel to know that you're not a challenge to God?

_____

_____

_____

_____

_____

_____

_____

_____

_____

_____

_____

_____

_____

_____

_____

_____

_____

_____

_____

_____

2. How does that thought challenge an old mindset?

_____

_____

_____

_____

_____

_____

_____

_____

_____

_____

_____

_____

_____

_____

_____

_____

_____

_____

_____

_____

_____

_____

_____

_____

_____

_____

_____

_____

3. What is a new, more brilliant thought you'd like to have about that instead?

_____
_____
_____
_____
_____
_____
_____
_____
_____
_____
_____
_____
_____
_____
_____
_____
_____
_____
_____
_____
_____
_____
_____
_____
_____
_____
_____
_____
_____

4. What upgrade is now possible in your relationship with Him?

"People become stuck because they have not seen what I see."

1. Where in your character would you like to become unstuck?

_____
_____
_____
_____
_____
_____
_____
_____
_____
_____
_____
_____
_____
_____
_____
_____
_____
_____
_____
_____
_____
_____
_____
_____
_____
_____

2. In standing with God, how would His perspective about this be different than yours?

_____

_____

_____

_____

_____

_____

_____

_____

_____

_____

_____

_____

_____

_____

_____

_____

_____

_____

_____

_____

_____

_____

_____

_____

_____

_____

_____

3. What freedom does He see ahead for you?

_____

_____

_____

_____

_____

_____

_____

_____

_____

_____

_____

_____

_____

_____

_____

_____

_____

_____

_____

_____

_____

_____

_____

_____

_____

_____

_____

_____

_____

_____

_____

_____

4. Describe how it feels to walk with Him towards that outcome.

"You must know the difference between what is true in your lifestyle and what is the Truth in Me. It may be true that you have a sin habit, but the Truth is that you are a new creation in Christ."

1. What Truth in this letter has brought you greater liberty?

_____

_____

_____

_____

_____

_____

_____

_____

_____

_____

_____

_____

_____

_____

_____

_____

_____

_____

_____

_____

_____

_____

_____

_____

2. What lies does it cut you free from?

_____

_____

_____

_____

_____

_____

_____

_____

_____

_____

_____

_____

_____

_____

_____

_____

_____

_____

_____

_____

_____

_____

_____

_____

_____

3. Is there a sin habit or lesser thought that it will help you overcome?

4. How does the Holy Spirit want to be your Helper and/or Comforter in that process?

_____

_____

_____

_____

_____

_____

_____

_____

_____

_____

_____

_____

_____

_____

_____

_____

_____

_____

_____

_____

_____

_____

_____

_____

_____

_____

_____

_____

INVITATION TO RESPOND

"We want you to be awestruck at what We are doing in you!"

Your last letter can express your praise, rejoicing and thanksgiving for how these letters from God have impacted your heart and your mind. What are you awestruck about? What new discoveries did you make? Share your dreams for what comes next in your relationship with Him. Then listen for His response.

_____

_____

_____

_____

_____

_____

_____

_____

_____

_____

_____

_____

_____

_____

_____

_____

_____

_____

_____

_____

_____

Graham Cooke

He is so delighted that you've engaged in this Divine Conversation and He has every intention of continuing it.

FINAL APPLICATION:
EVIDENCES OF TRANSFORMATION

Your stories of personal transformation are the true mile markers on your journey.

Evidences of Transformation are not a one time experience, but a continuing conversation with God and any group of friends you may be sharing this journey with.

EVIDENCE OF TRANSFORMATION IN PERCEPTION:
HOW WE SEE AND PERCEIVE THE WORLD AROUND US

I am viewing every circumstance as an opportunity to practice what I am learning about God's true nature of freedom.

"Before, I would have _____. Now I often _____.

Give one real life example of this:

_____

_____

_____

_____

_____

_____

_____

_____

_____

_____

_____

_____

_____

_____

_____

_____

_____

_____

_____

_____

_____

_____

_____

_____

EVIDENCE OF TRANSFORMATION IN MINDSETS:
HOW WE THINK ABOUT WHAT WE'RE PERCEIVING

I am thinking more present-future, considering the new creation I am in Christ rather than focusing on self-improving my old nature.

"Instead of _____ I am now _____."

Give one real life example of this:

_____

_____

_____

_____

_____

_____

_____

_____

_____

_____

_____

_____

_____

_____

_____

_____

_____

_____

_____

_____

EVIDENCE OF TRANSFORMATION IN LANGUAGE: HOW WE TALK ABOUT OURSELVES, GOD AND OTHERS

I no longer talk about what's wrong with myself or others, but rather what is missing in my experience of God. My language reflects my confidence in His provision of it.

"Instead of speaking about _____, I now choose to express it by _____.

Give one real life example of this:

_____

_____

_____

_____

_____

_____

_____

_____

_____

_____

_____

_____

_____

_____

_____

_____

_____

_____

_____

_____

EVIDENCE OF TRANSFORMATION IN ACTIONS:
OUR CHOICES IN BEHAVIOR

I am encountering God's empowering presence to better perceive my true identity in Christ and then behave or respond to others accordingly.

"Rather than choosing to _____, I am choosing to because I realize _____."

Give one real life example of this:

_____

_____

_____

_____

_____

_____

_____

_____

_____

_____

_____

_____

_____

_____

_____

_____

_____

_____

_____

_____

FOLLOW THROUGH YOUR BREAKTHROUGHS

There are two battles over every new territory: the first to take ground and the second to hold it. There is no lasting breakthrough without follow through. Consider these opportunities to further explore and establish what The Nature of Freedom has opened up for you.

Revisit, reread and revise

These journals are not meant to be a one time experience. Engage with the questions every time you read and note how your answers change.

Create your own "Evidences of Transformation"

What other areas of perception, thinking, language and actions are encountering transformation? What truths are upgrading from what you believe to becoming your lifestyle?

Focus on one key truth at a time

Choose one key truth to write on a small card. Post it where you'll see it often. Is there a photograph you could partner with it? Start a journal of your conversations with the Holy Spirit and enjoy exploring one truth deeply.

Continue your correspondence

This journal provides letter writing practice that you can continue with God about any of the truths that captivate your heart or challenge your thinking. Listen for His joy-filled replies about who you are and are becoming and continue the conversation.

Additional Notes:

_____

_____

_____

_____

_____

_____

_____

_____

_____

_____

_____

_____

_____

_____

_____

_____

_____

_____

_____

_____

_____

_____

_____

_____

_____

_____

_____

_____

_____

_____

_____

Coming soon...

BOOK 2:

The Newness

Advantage

THE LETTERS FROM GOD SERIES

Exploring the real, true you in Jesus and all the blessing, favor and upgrades that are made available to us in our new nature in Christ. This book powerfully explores these topics:

Seeing yourself in Jesus

Living the life He creates

Making war on negativity

Unclaimed upgrades

Elevating the Gospel to the place God always intended.

Available early 2017 at www.BrilliantBookHouse.com

ABOUT THE AUTHOR

Graham and Theresa Cooke reside in Santa Barbara, California. Working together with their closest friends they have formed a Kingdom community called Radiance. Radiance is a community of creatives and entrepreneurs with a citywide focus on Arts and Business. While individual members of the community are involved in a wide range of Kingdom activities (i.e. caring for the poor, teaching/training, pastoral ministry) the community, as a whole, is focused on impacting the social pillars of Arts and Business in Santa Barbara. They are committed to making a place for Kingdom-minded dreamers to explore and realize the potential of their imagination—and to raising the "water level" of Kingdom Culture in this city.

He is married to Theresa who has a passion for worship and dance. She loves to be involved in intercession, warfare and setting people free. She cares about injustice, abuse and has compassion for people who are sick, suffering and disenfranchised.

Graham and Theresa have a growing family spanning two generations and several countries. All their children are involved in business, the arts and entertainment. There are numerous grandchildren who keep them busy laughing and enjoying life.

Graham is a popular conference speaker and is well known for his training programs on the prophetic, spiritual warfare, intimacy and devotional life, leadership, spirituality and the church in transition. He functions as a consultant and freethinker to businesses, churches and organizations, enabling them to develop strategically. He has a passion to establish the Kingdom and build prototype churches that can fully reach a post-modern society.

A strong part of Graham's ministry is in producing finances and resources for the poor and disenfranchised in developing countries. He supports many projects specifically for widows, orphans and people in the penal system. He hates the abuse of women and works actively against human trafficking and the sex slave trade; including women caught up in prostitution and pornography.

Graham is an ambassador for communities of faith in the Body of Christ on behalf of Not For Sale. He talks about the work of Not For Sale and empowers individuals, families, businesses, ministries and churches to get involved in sponsoring projects. Not For Sale have specific assignments that involve rescue, restoration and providing education; skills-based training and small business development to enable people to become fully rehabilitated into a normal, productive life.

If you would like to invite Graham to minister at an event, please complete our online Ministry Invitation Form at BrilliantPerspectives.com.

If you want to give to Not For Sale and partner with them directly, it's simple. Go to their website, NotForSaleCampaign.org.

Look at the range of what they are doing and at the very least give a one time gift, or give a monthly donation for six months or one year. Better still; involve your family, friends, business or church in sponsoring a specific project.

Your contribution makes a world of difference to the people rescued by your involvement.

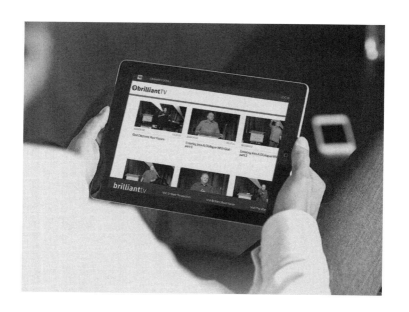

brilliantTV.com

access a growing video library of
teachings by Graham Cooke for one low
monthly subscription

optimized for mobile devices
available anywhere with internet or network connection

NOT FOR SALE

Not For Sale protects people and communities around the world from modern-day slavery and human trafficking.

Through business, education, job training, providing homes, long-term care, health & rescue, legal support, and rehabilitation.

GOODNESS IN ACTION, POWERFULLY!

BRILLIANT is honored to act as an Ambassador for this great organization, by raising funds and awareness.

END SLAVERY NOW! Your help matters.

www.notforsalecampaign.org